Mike&Scrabble

A guide to training your new Human

By Scrabble, as dictated to Mike Dicks

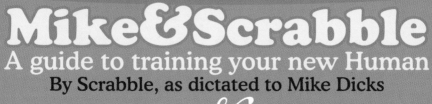

Hubble&Hattie

www.hubbleandhattie.com   www.mikeandscrabble.com

The Hubble & Hattie imprint was launched in 2009 and is named in memory of two very special Westie sisters owned by Veloce's proprietors. Since the first book, many more have been added to the list, all with the same underlying objective: to be of real benefit to the species they cover, at the same time promoting compassion, understanding and respect between all animals (including human ones!)

All Hubble & Hattie publications offer ethical, high quality content and presentation, plus great value for money.

You might also enjoy these Hubble and Hattie books –

Boating with Buster –
the life and times of a barge Beagle
(Alderton)

Bonds –
Capturing the special relationship that
dogs share with their people
(Cukuraite & Pais)

Charlie –
The dog who came in from the wild
(Tenzin-Dolma)

For the love of Scout –
promises to a small dog
(Ison)

Gods, ghosts, and black dogs –
the fascinating folklore and mythology of dogs
(Coren)

Hounds who heal –
people and dogs: it's a kind of magic
(Kent)

My Dog, my Friend –
heart-warming tales of canine companionship from
celebrities and other extraordinary people
(Gordon)

Tara –
the terrier who sailed around the world
(Forrester)

Unleashing the healing power of animals –
True stories about therapy animals – and what they do for us
(Preece-Kelly)

When man meets dog –
what a difference a dog makes
(Blazina)

Winston ... the dog who changed my life
(Klute)

The quite very actual adventures of Worzel Wooface
(Pickles)

Worzel Wooface – The quite very actual Terribibble Twos
(Pickles)

For post publication news, updates and
amendments relating to this book please visit
www.hubbleandhattie.com/extras/HH5000

www.hubbleandhattie.com

First published February 2017 by Veloce Publishing Limited, Veloce House, Parkway Farm Business Park, Middle Farm Way, Poundbury, Dorchester, Dorset, DT1 3AR, England. Fax 01305 250479/email info@hubbleandhattie.com/web www.hubbleandhattie.com ISBN: 978-1-78711-000-7 UPC: 6-36847-01000-3

Readers with ideas for books about animals, or animal-related topics, are invited to write to the editorial director of Veloce Publishing at the above address. British Library Cataloguing in Publication Data - A catalogue record for this book is available from the British Library. Typesetting, design and page make-up all by Mike Dicks. Mike has used Cooper Black and Cooper MD throughout the book, because he claims he wants to 'make them cool' again. Printed in India by Replika Press.

Thank you for buying this silly book.
By doing so you have contributed to these
wonderful charities that helped Mike&Scrabble

Dedication
For Foxy, Rolo and Laika

www.hubbleandhattie.com

Mike&Scrabble

www.mikeandscrabble.com
@mikeandscrabble
www.facebook.com/MikeAndScrabble

Foreword

We asked a famous Human to write some nice things about us

Liz Fraser

Humans are strange creatures.

We come in all shapes and sizes, characters and traits – almost different breeds. Much like dogs, in fact.

I've known the Human who wrote this book for twenty years. He is a true mongrel – a crazy, unique crossbreed somewhere between a terrier, a sheepdog, a Beagle and a caffeinated Meerkat – determined, loyal, energetic, stubborn, funny, clever, and most definitely bonkers.

Mike doesn't belong in a box; if there is one, he will think, and be, outside it. To him, the whole world is a playground: a mystery, something to prod and explore, dig about in and bury stuff for safekeeping until another day, when this Brilliant Idea will be rediscovered and played with again.

Sometimes humans lose themselves in the messy path of life, especially when they like to stray off-piste. When this happens it generally takes an observant, honest eye to show us the way again.

Children often do this. And so can our most faithful of friends: dogs. In the Mike/Scrabble partnership, Scrabble is most definitely the owner. She takes Mike on walks, shows him stuff, pushes him to question and re-evaluate things, see the world in a new light, and find his way again.

The cartoons Mike draws of his friendship with Scrabble are beautiful, whimsical, clever and highly observant – and through Scrabble's simple animal point-of-view and humour, reveal more about us as humans than most humans could.

Philosophy meets psychology meets counselling – Mike and Scrabble are the perfect partnership to laugh at our faults, idiocy and general human incompetence – and learn how to live and love again.

Liz Fraser is one of the UK's best-known writers and broadcasters on all aspects of modern family life, a social commentator, presenter, columnist, podcaster, comedy writer and performer. She appears frequently on national TV and radio, from ITV1's *This Morning* and *Good Morning Britain* to Sky News, BBC Breakfast, LBC radio, BBC 5Live, Channel 5 News, and many others.

Foreword

Not satisfied with that, we asked another famous Human to write some nice things about us

Michelle Gayle

What can I tell you about Mike?

Well, I could tell you about the time we had four weeks to write and deliver an important pitch at Blackberry HQ, only for Mike to start it the day before the meeting and absolutely knock it out the ballpark on the day!

Or I could tell you about the time he spent six weeks doodling his way through a writing course we were doing, to then end up delivering the best script of the term.

I wouldn't be surprised if he wrote this book yesterday.

In short, he is infuriatingly talented! I do, however, always beat him at Scrabble so how he has the cheek to associate the good game with his name I'll never know, but I'm guessing he has probably conquered that, too.

PS I'm actually more of a cat person myself, but through his social media posts, and now this book, Mike has managed to make me fall in love with his dog – such are his writing skills.

Witty, clever and funny: if he wasn't my friend I'd probably hate him!

Michelle Gayle is a British recording artist, songwriter, actress and author. Michelle had success as a Soul and R&B singer in the 1990s. She achieved seven Top 40 singles in the UK Singles Chart, her two biggest hits to date being *Sweetness* and *Do You Know*

As an actress, Gayle is best known for her work on television, in particular playing Fiona Wilson in *Grange Hill*, Hattie Tavernier in *EastEnders*, and Imara Ciprani in *Wolfblood*.

Michelle branched into writing and the rights to her first novel were acquired by Walker Books in 2010. The book, *Pride and Premiership*, was published on 5 May 2011. In 2016 Michelle wrote scripts for the BBC series *Wolfblood*.

Mike

Hello! my name is Mike, I am a loser and I live in Brighton, well, actually I live in Hove but nobody knows where that is, so we'll call it Brighton. I share a flat with a dog called Scrabble, on the roof of an old factory on a street that winds down to the sea front.

When I was a kid I always wanted to be an artist. I started as I meant to go on by failing my Art O'Level twice, so I became a salesman instead.

Variously, I sold televisions and cameras, photocopiers and fax machines, cornflakes, slacks and hand-dryers. Luckily, I was very good at getting jobs, because I was also an expert at losing them.

I married my school sweetheart, and we made two children – one of each – a smart one and a clever one.

Accidentally, I learnt to make television programmes, and whilst I did that I tripped over the internet when it was as young and stupid as I.

I got divorced from my school sweetheart, which was awful, and I moved to a flat in London Zoo, well, actually it was in Camden but nobody knows where that is, so we'll call it a Zoo.

After expertly losing some more jobs, I learnt to teach instead of do, and I travelled the world talking rubbish to people and getting paid to do so. Then I met a Perfect Human and I proposed to her in Africa, and then married her in a garden tent. We exchanged gifts – I gave her problems, she gave me grace, hope and a new family.

I stopped getting jobs, because I had become too good at losing them, so instead I got cancer – which is much more difficult to misplace. When my Perfect Human's daughter also became ill, we got a dog called Rolo to help us both get well; then I lost Rolo.

Because I am good at losing things, I lost my cancer last year, well, technically I've misplaced it for a few years, but I also managed to misplace my Perfect Human, for a while, and I moved to Brighton (well, Hove) to find my health and myself. When I got here I found Scrabble, well, she found me, really. I started to draw pictures of Scrabble and Brighton and I shared them on Twitter and Facebook, and I found some nice people who asked if they could buy them, in frames, for their walls, and I became an artist.

Then a nice lady called Jude found Scrabble and I in a corner of the internet. Jude asked if she could make a book of our pictures, which you've just found. Try not to lose it.

Mike

Hello, my name is Scrabble, I live in Hove, not Brighton, with a Human called Mike. Mike is a loveable human and I love him, though I don't think he knows why.

When I was a pup I wanted to be an author.

I started life on a puppy farm in Ireland. My father was a cheeky Jack Russell who snuck into the Dachshund dorm one night and I was the result – the farm owner called me an 'accident' but I prefer Jackshund.

One winter's night I rather abruptly left the farm, when a truck from Battersea Dogs Home came to collect me, and a bunch of other accidents, to take us to London.

I didn't mind too much as London is the place where authors are made, plus the farmer had stopped feeding us some time ago.

London wasn't what I expected, so I took a holiday in the Sussex Downs at an exclusive writers' retreat called The Allsorts Rescue Centre.

As part of their package Allsorts choose a nom de plume for dogs wishing to write books, and I arrived in a week that the theme for these names was board games. I narrowly escaped being called Monopoly and settled on the more intellectual-sounding Scrabble instead.

I whiled away the days chatting to other dogs and running around the fields outside our accommodation. As part of the programme humans would come to visit the resort and we would take them for a short walk.

One day a Human called Mike visited, a scruffy-looking mongrel, but with an endearing smile, and I was at once both smitten by him and felt pity for him.

I took Mike for a walk up the winding, tree-lined lane to the top of the hill above the resort, and sat him on a bench as he told me his story and asked me for help. Then and there, I decided to put off my aspirations to be a writer – I had been experiencing some difficulty holding a pen anyway – and make it my mission to train Mike to be a better Human.

This book is my attempt to share my experiences of training Mike with other dogs who adopt humans. They can be exasperatingly dumb creatures, but they are worth the effort if you find a good one.

Always remember that no matter how gloomy
your Human gets — it is YOU who saved him,
not the other way round

Let's start with a story about Blood Cancer,
dead dogs and, most importantly,
how Scrabble came to own Mike

A year or so ago, Mike started getting pains in his neck; bad pains that just wouldn't go away

Mike's vet, Anna, told him he had Leukaemia —
a type of Blood Cancer that takes away
your immune system and slows you down

While Mike was still waiting for his cancer to get worse, before he could get some treatment, he was rescued by a dog, called Rolo, who walked him

Sadly, Rolo was killed when she ran off to chase a deer (this is the dead dog bit)

Not long after Rolo died, Mike got worse
and his vet said it was time for chemotherapy

After 6 months of IVs and pills and generally being gloomy, Mike's vet gave him the 'All Clear.' His cancer had gone, for now; it wouldn't come back for a few years

And that's when Mike moved to Brighton
where Scrabble found him and decided to help him
get fit again and give him something to draw

So is the moral of this story that
Anna or Rolo were great*?
No, it's that every human deserves to
be owned by a dog

(* they were)

If your Human shows any signs of cancer,
send him to the Human Vet — otherwise
you might lose your source of food and walks

Humans need to be constantly reminded
that you are willing to eat their food

Encourage your Human to take you to the pub.
It is likely he will drop a kebab on the way home

Just before they go to bed, your Human may
want to watch you wee in the garden ...
this is because he is a pervert

At bedtime, your Human will find it
reassuring to be barked to sleep

Humans love cleaning their cars:
give them a real challenge by
being sick every time he puts you in his

Ensure your Human keeps his home clean
by regularly shedding all your hair

Make sure all floors are kept disinfected
by weeing on them every day

Never perform a 'trick' in the way
your Human wants. It just plays to their ego,
and you'll get the snack anyway

If you are unhappy with your bed
let your Human know by eating it
when he is out shopping

Do not bark at the Amazon delivery man ...
He could be bringing you new shoes to eat

If your Human has separation anxiety when you visit the Dog-Sitter, pretend you prefer being with him, rather than there

Teach your Human how dangerous roads are
by pooing on a zebra crossing

Encourage a false sense of security
in your Human, by waiting at least a
week before having another 'accident'

Your Human will enjoy playing the
"you hang 'em up, I'll pull 'em down"
laundry game

Humans are very sensitive to sunlight.
If you find a sunny spot on your balcony
keep it for yourself, for their protection

It is not safe for your Human to go out alone;
if it happens, alert the neighbours
by barking incessantly

If your Human asks you to eat his homework
it is likely you are being used as an excuse

Humans don't put leads on Cats
because they don't care if a Cat runs away

Avoid losing your Human in public
by tying him up with your lead

Although you shouldn't show any favouritism,
some Humans are obviously better than others

Human 'Cool' is relative.
Compared to his best friend,
your Human is not 'Cool'

Your Human will always appreciate a face-lick,
especially when he knows where
your tongue has just been

If your Human gets a new favourite shirt
accept the fact that you'll not be going for a walk
till he's drawn it

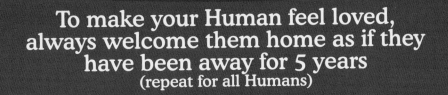

To make your Human feel loved,
always welcome them home as if they
have been away for 5 years
(repeat for all Humans)

It is often a good idea to remind your Human that despite the unconditional love thing you could also eat him

Your Human will indicate that he wants you to squeeze in between him and his wife, by sitting on the sofa with his arm around her

Humans do not have a good sense of smell;
to them Fox Poo smells of Poo instead of
Chanel No.5

If your Human suggests a trip in a space rocket
ask him to show you the re-entry plans

Humans like simple games; he will never get
bored with throwing the ball when you
fetch it for him

There are some days when your Human will feel glum and like he's shot himself in the foot. On these days only unconditional LOVE will help

Sometimes you might have to make your
Human sit on the naughty step

If your Human puts on a suit and leaves you
extra food, it is highly likely that you are
not going out with him tonight

Your Human will often wash you in a 'bath' but he may still object to you washing him with a face-lick. This is because he really does know where your tongue has just been

While he is out, check your Human's search history
to see if he's been looking at other dogs online

Humans do not really understand
Canine Social Media

It doesn't matter how many Facebook 'friends'
your Human has, you are still his BEST friend

If you'd rather walk than use public transport try weeing on your Human's lap when he takes you on the bus

Mike isn't the only one with famous friends,
Scrabble recently met Worzel Wooface
who is quite "fabumazingly" tall!

It is not worth trying to explain to your Human that 'Scoobee' has no concept of how to "Get a Room!"

After a few hours of playing "Where did you bury my f***!ng keys?" your Human will grow tired of the game and start to cry

Unlike dogs, humans don't know
how to live in the moment

If your Human is offered a book deal
make sure it's him and not you who
has to do the book signings

Sometimes your Human just
needs you to listen to him

Your Human will make many mistakes in life;
getting a dog is not one of them ...